FANDOM FEVER

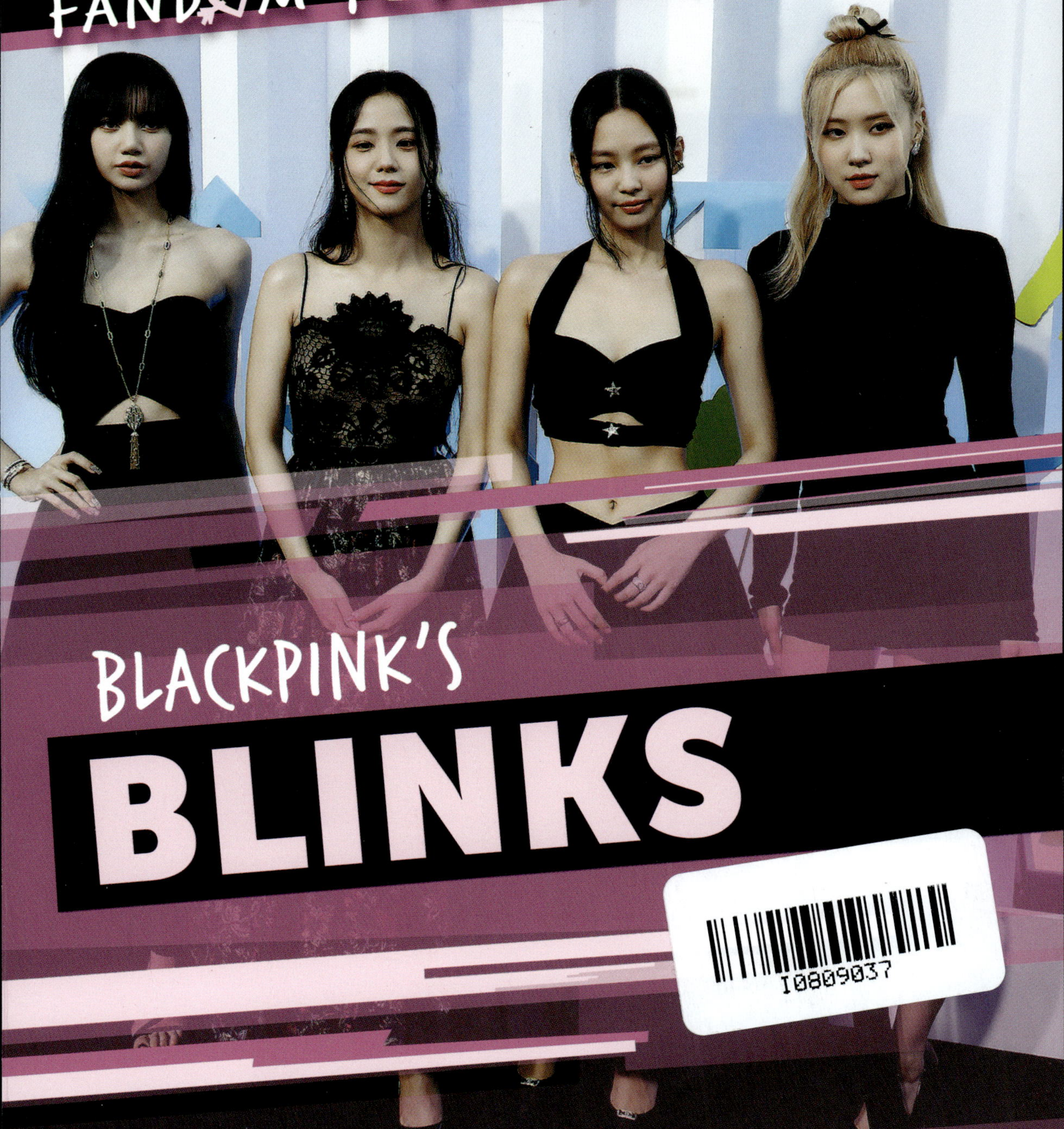

BLACKPINK'S BLINKS

BY VIRGINIA LOH-HAGAN

45TH PARALLEL PRESS

Published in the United States of America by
Cherry Lake Publishing Group
Ann Arbor, Michigan
www.cherrylakepublishing.com

Reading Adviser: Beth Walker Gambro, MS, Ed., Reading Consultant, Yorkville, IL
Book Designer: Joseph Hatch

Photo Credits: © ZUMA Press, Inc./Alamy Stock Photo, cover, title page; © JTMJA/Shutterstock, 4; © JuliaDorian/Shutterstock, 7; © Everyonephoto Studio/Shutterstock, 8; © Imaginechina Limited/Alamy Stock Photo, 11; © taniavolobueva/Shutterstock, 12; PUBG MOBILE: 絕地求生M, CC BY 3.0 via Wikimedia Commons, 13; © David Skinner, CC BY 2.0 via Wikimedia Commons, 14; © Steve Bower/Shutterstock, 17; Explicit, CC BY-SA 4.0 via Wikimedia Commons, 19; © MediaPunch Inc/Alamy Stock Photo, 21; © yllyso/Shutterstock, 22; © Imaginechina Limited/Alamy Stock Photo, 25; © Nawatat/Shutterstock, 26; Samsonite Red, CC BY-SA 4.0 via Wikimedia Commons, 29; Marie Claire Korea, CC BY 3.0 via Wikimedia Commons, 31

45th Parallel Press is an imprint of Cherry Lake Publishing Group.

Library of Congress Cataloging-in-Publication Data

Names: Loh-Hagan, Virginia, author.
Title: Blackpink's Blinks / Virginia Loh-Hagan.
Description: Ann Arbor : 45th Parallel Press, 2024. | Series: Fandom fever | Audience: Grades 4-6 | Summary: "Blackpink's BLINKS provides an inside look at the powerful fandom of Blackpink. Readers will get hooked on this hi-lo title, covering facts about and insights into the group of fans who aren't afraid to make their support of this K-pop girl group known"— Provided by publisher.
Identifiers: LCCN 2024009450 | ISBN 9781668947456 (hardcover) | ISBN 9781668948842 (paperback) | ISBN 9781668950364 (ebook) | ISBN 9781668954928 (pdf)
Subjects: LCSH: Blackpink (Musical group)—Juvenile literature. | Popular music fans—Juvenile literature.
Classification: LCC ML3930.B579 L+ | DDC 782.4216/3095195—dc23/eng/20240227
LC record available at https://lccn.loc.gov/2024009450

Cherry Lake Publishing Group would like to acknowledge the work of the Partnership for 21st Century Learning, a Network of Battelle for Kids. Please visit Battelle for Kids online for more information.

Note from publisher: Websites change regularly, and their future contents are outside of our control. Supervise children when conducting any recommended online searches for extended learning opportunities.

Printed in the United States of America

Table of Contents

Dr. Virginia Loh-Hagan is an author and educator. She is currently the Director of the Asian Pacific Islander Desi American (APIDA) Center at San Diego State University and the Co-Executive Director of The Asian American Education Project. She lives in San Diego with her very tall husband and very naughty dogs.

BLACKPINK FOR LIFE!

For a fan, seeing their favorite artists on tour is the best! It helps them get close to their idols.

CHAPTER ONE

From Fan Base to Fandom

Musicians make music. They perform music. Some become big stars. They become **celebrities**. Celebrities are famous. They have a **fan base**. A fan base is a group of supporters.

Most fans have a casual interest. But some fans are more devoted. They worship their **idols**. Idols are big stars. Devoted fans form **fandoms**. Fandoms are communities. They're networks of fans.

Fandoms of musicians are special groups. They buy the musicians' music. They buy their **merch**. Merch means merchandise. It means stuff that can be sold. Merch includes shirts and posters. Fans follow musicians on tour. They attend their shows. They go on tour with them. They connect with the music. They connect with the messages. They sing their songs. They know all the words.

Fandoms are a powerful force. They can influence music. They use the internet. The internet gives fans information about their idols. It gives them more access to their idols. It also gives them more access to other fans.

Fans build relationships with each other. They share their knowledge. They share their passion. They build connections. They create content. They share content.

Fans make fan art. This is when they draw pictures of their idols. Fans also write stories about their idols. This is called fan fiction. They share their art. They share their stories.

Some celebrities have large fandoms. Their fandoms even have special names. That's a sign of success!

Many arists come out with special editions of their albums. Their fans love this!

Many K-pop groups have photocards.
Fans like to collect them.

CHAPTER TWO

Fanning Blackpink

Blackpink is a South Korean girl band. They're the world's biggest girl group. They're a leading force in **K-pop**. Today, there's great interest in South Korean pop culture. K-pop includes music. It includes movies. It includes beauty products.

Blackpink formed in 2016. They **debuted** with the single album *Square One*. Debut means first appearance. They quickly rose in fame. The band members are Jisoo, Jennie, Rosé, and Lisa.

Blackpink is a combination of 2 words. Black refers to being edgy. Girls can be both cute and confident. Pink refers to their **feminine** side. Feminine means womanly. Blackpink members say they're girly and **savage** at the same time. Savage means tough. It means fierce.

Pink usually refers to pretty and cute. But black adds an edge. So Blackpink means that pretty isn't everything. It means its members have talent as well.

Blackpink songs are top hits. The band performs all around the world. Their shows sell out. They always have big crowds. They have sold many albums. They've won many awards. They're loved by many.

Their fandom is known as Blink. Blink combines two words. The two words are Black and Pink. Blink uses the beginning of Black. It uses the end of Pink. This means fans are with Blackpink from beginning to end. It means they'll be together forever.

Blackpink has a song called "Pretty Savage." It describes them best.

SUPER FAN

Usher is an American singer. He's also a dancer. He's sold many records. He's also a Blink. He loves Blackpink. He has 2 teen sons. He took his kids to see Blackpink. The show was in Atlanta, Georgia. It was part of the Born Pink World Tour. It's the biggest tour for a girl group in K-pop history. Blackpink performed in 14 North American cities. Usher said the show was amazing. He said, "They were putting on a show. Wardrobe. Great sequencing. With the lighting. And, everything working in sync. There's no detail spared. I loved that." There were different themes. There were fireworks. There were bursts of confetti. Confetti is colorful bits of paper. Usher was impressed with Blackpink. *GQ* magazine said he "took notes in his head." This means he wants to learn from them.

The Blink fandom launched in 2016. Blackpink posted a picture on their Instagram. The posting was black. It had the word "Blink" on it. The letters were in pink. The "N" was backward. There was no **caption**. Captions describe pictures. Fans guessed what it meant. Blackpink's fandom was born.

Blinks are all over the world. They form smaller online groups. They promote the band. They plan ways to increase their views. They work to keep Blackpink at the top of the charts. A fan said, "We are doing it because we want Blackpink to know that we do appreciate the music. And, that we recognize their hard work."

Blackpink members like edgy fashion. They like casual styles too. They wear designer clothes.

Blackpink did the Born Pink World Tour in 2023. They did 66 concerts. They went to 22 countries.

CHAPTER THREE

Living That Fan Life

Blinks show up at Blackpink events. To be a Blink, make sure to look the part! Do the following:

- Study Blackpink's looks. Copy their style. Crop tops are popular. Short skirts are popular. Some Blinks **cosplay** as their favorite member. Cosplay means to dress in costume.

- Get Blackpink's light stick. It lights up during shows. It syncs to the music. It's shaped like a hammer. It's black and pink. It has striped pink hearts. It makes a squeaky sound.

- Wear Blackpink jewelry. This includes necklaces, bracelets, and rings. They have Blackpink's name on them.

- Wear sparkly makeup. Some Blackpink members wear face gems. These gems are sparkly stickers. They're placed at the ends of eyes. They're placed across noses. They're placed on cheeks.

Blinks have their own culture. To be a Blink, make sure to act the part! Do the following:

+ Buy photocards. They are like playing cards. They have pictures of Blackpink. They can be traded. They can be stored in a photobook.

+ Watch *Blackpink: The Movie.* The movie was made in 2021. It's about the band. It features each band member. It has interviews. It has performances. Gather other Blinks. Host a movie-watching party.

+ Learn how to use social media. Blinks make rules about streaming Blackpink music. Fans follow them. They increase Blackpink's listeners. They make sure Blackpink has tons of support.

Vietnamese Blinks hosted "Pink up the Sky." Hot air balloons with plenty of pink welcomed the band to Vietnam.

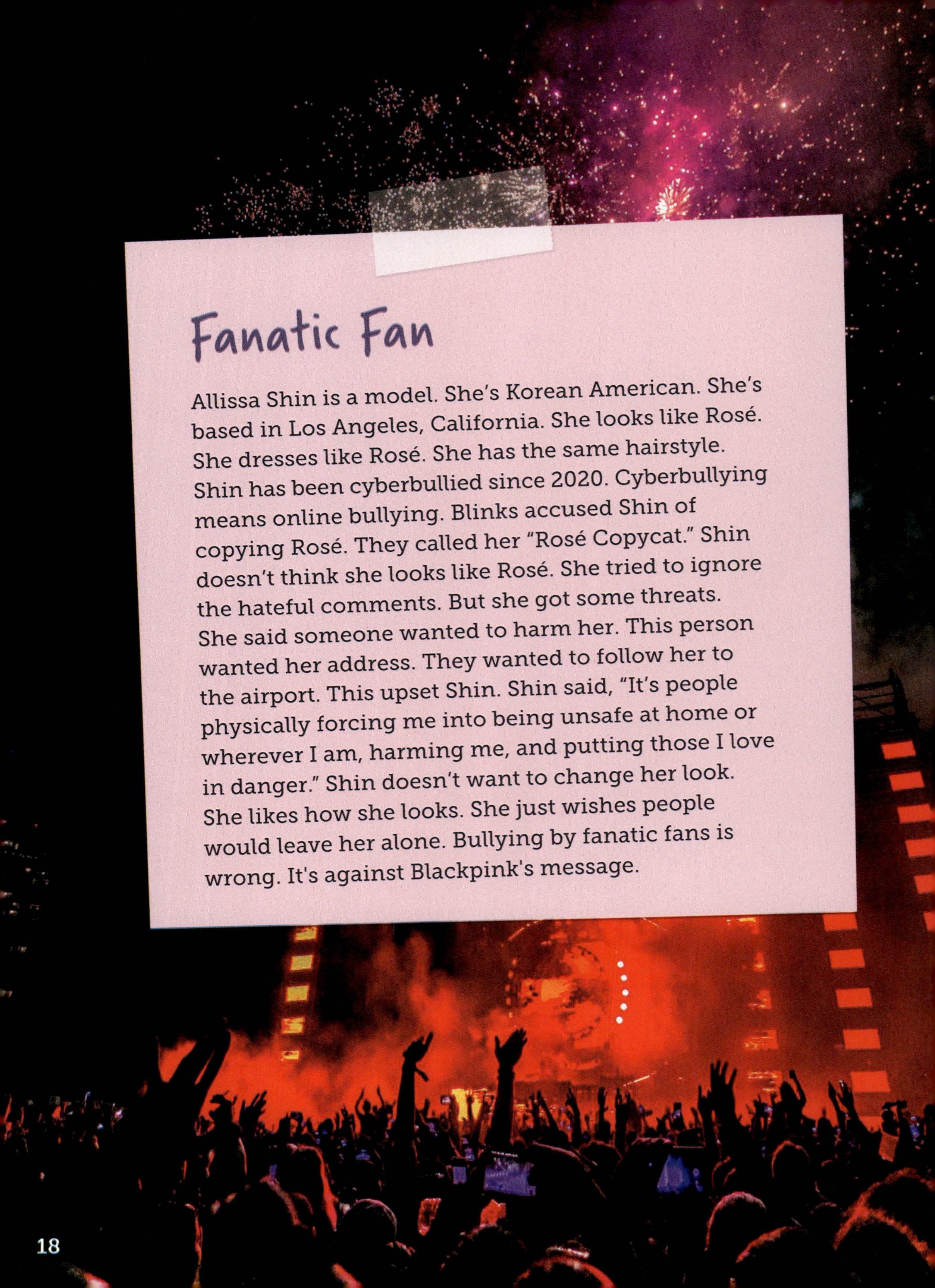

Fanatic Fan

Allissa Shin is a model. She's Korean American. She's based in Los Angeles, California. She looks like Rosé. She dresses like Rosé. She has the same hairstyle. Shin has been cyberbullied since 2020. Cyberbullying means online bullying. Blinks accused Shin of copying Rosé. They called her "Rosé Copycat." Shin doesn't think she looks like Rosé. She tried to ignore the hateful comments. But she got some threats. She said someone wanted to harm her. This person wanted her address. They wanted to follow her to the airport. This upset Shin. Shin said, "It's people physically forcing me into being unsafe at home or wherever I am, harming me, and putting those I love in danger." Shin doesn't want to change her look. She likes how she looks. She just wishes people would leave her alone. Bullying by fanatic fans is wrong. It's against Blackpink's message.

Not all fan behavior is good. Some fans can be **toxic**. Toxic means harmful. In Korea, toxic fans are called **sasaeng**. To be a Blink, don't let your passion become poison. Do the following:

+ Respect Blackpink's privacy. Toxic fans have stalked them.

+ Avoid Blonks. Blonks are fake Blinks. They pretend to be Blinks. They make fake fan accounts. They say bad things. They bash the band. They bash fans. They're haters.

+ Don't make fun of other K-pop groups. Some Blinks have sent death threats. They make nasty comments. They bully others.

People have a right to live their lives. Focus on the art more than the artist.

Blackpink at a fan event in South Korea

CHAPTER FOUR

The Power of Fandom

Blinks are inspired by their idols. They support them. They support their causes. Together, they're a powerful force. They've helped people. They've made social changes.

Blackpink cares about **climate change**. Climate change is the warming of the planet. It harms life. Blackpink made a video in 2021. They shared what they learned about climate change. They asked world leaders to protect Earth. They said, "Let's work together for our planet. And take climate action in your area." This inspired fans. Blinks started #ClimateActionInYourArea. They planted trees. Trees help clean the air. They help stop climate change.

The United Kingdom gave Blackpink an award.
It was for fighting climate change.

Blinks protect Blackpink. Blackpink is managed by a company named YG Entertainment. Some Blinks think YG doesn't promote the band enough. They think they're doing a bad job.

Blinks want Blackpink to have more songs. They organized a protest. They had a truck. The truck had a sign. The sign read, "Blink Demands for Blackpink." They drove past the YG building.

Toxic fans found where Blackpink member Jennie lived. They posted her address online. This is unsafe. Blinks organized for Jennie. They called themselves the "Jensetters Union." They drove trucks with signs. They went to YG. They wanted YG to protect Jennie.

The YG building is in Seoul. Seoul is in South Korea.

Idol Inspiration

Idols have idols. Blackpink loves Lady Gaga. Lady Gaga is an American singer and actress. She's famous for reinventing herself. She has a big fandom. Her fandom is called Little Monsters. Blackpink studied Lady Gaga. They did this before they were famous. They said they wanted to make "great music" like Lady Gaga. Jisoo said, "There are so many things to learn from Lady Gaga. She is not afraid to try new things." Lisa said, "I can't list all the influences that Lady Gaga has given me and my generation...I respect Lady Gaga's unique style and [the way] she makes her own music and performances. She is an artist who always creates new styles that have never been done before. And, she delivers meaningful messages to people who hear her music." Blackpink and Lady Gaga wrote a song together. This happened in 2020. The song is called "Sour Candy."

CHAPTER FIVE

Insider Information

Fans know their idols. They can also spot fake fans. Make sure you do your research. Here are the top 10 things every true Blink should know about Blackpink!

1. Blackpink was formed by YG Entertainment. Singers **auditioned**. Auditions are tryouts. YG chose members. At first, there were 9 members. Then there were the final 4. They were YG's first girl group.

2. Not all Blackpink members are from South Korea. Jisoo and Jennie are Korean. But Rosé is from New Zealand. And Lisa is from Thailand. They can all speak different languages.

3. Blackpink practices their dance moves. They post videos. They connect with their fans. They show how real they are.

Blackpink had other name choices. One was Pink Punk.

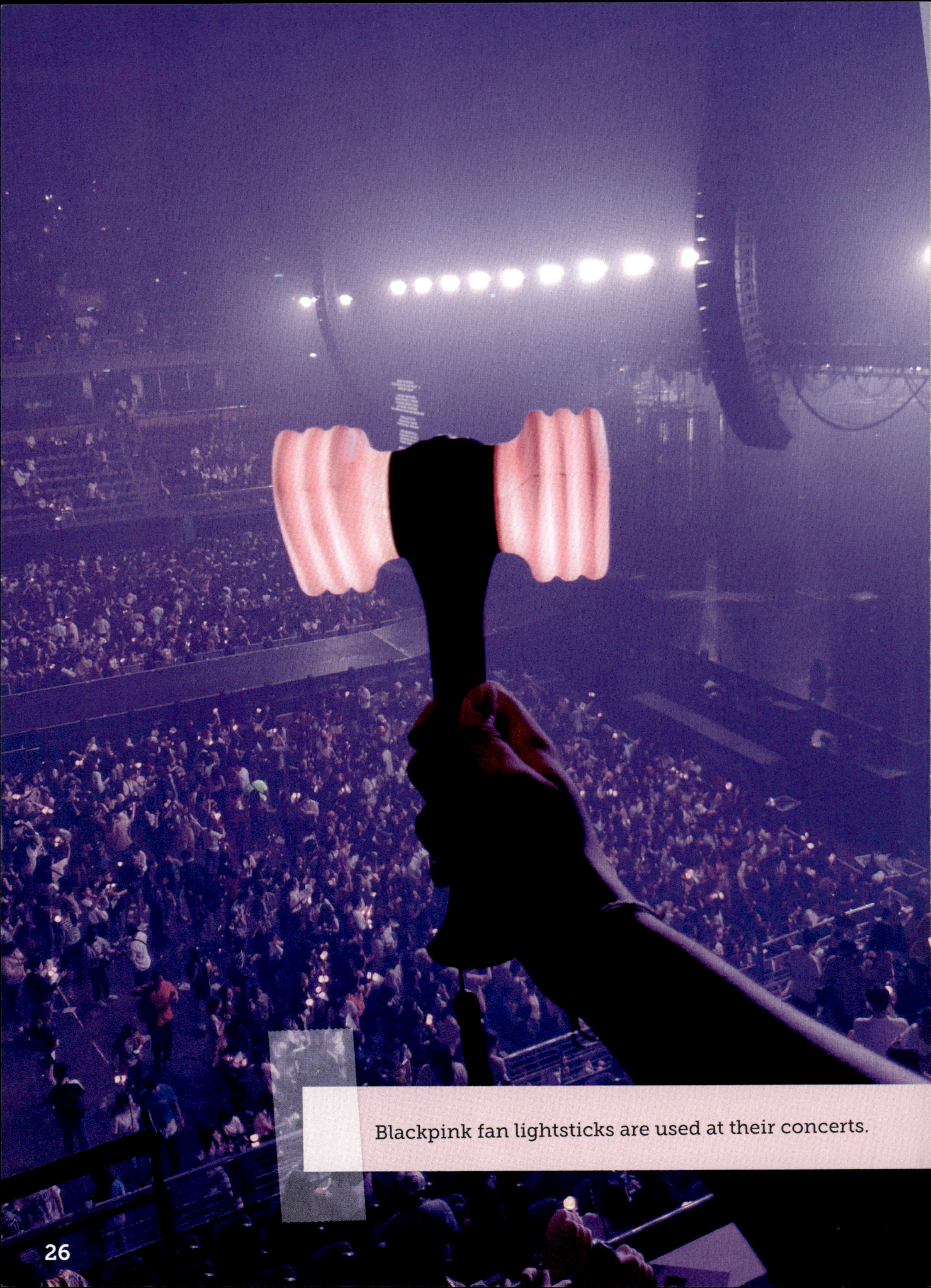

Blackpink fan lightsticks are used at their concerts.

4. Blackpink debuted with the single album *Square One* in 2016. It had the tracks "Whistle" and "Boombayah."

5. Blackpink had a reality show. This was in 2018. The show was called *Blackpink House*. It's about their lives. The girls lived together. They shared the same house.

6. Between 2016 and 2020, the band had about 13 songs. This is a limited number. Their star power is based on their stage performances. They're glamorous. They're good dancers. They include many themes in their music videos. They're exciting to watch.

7. Blackpink has many Japanese fans. They have recorded some songs in Japanese.

8. Blackpink has worked with other famous people. Their partners include Selena Gomez and Lady Gaga.

9. Each member has **solo** projects. Solo means by themselves. Jennie was the first to go solo. Each member has their own music. They model for different brands. They're famous as a group. They're also famous on their own.

10. Blackpink performed at Coachella. Coachella is a popular music festival. Blackpink is the first Korean act to headline. They did this in 2023. They also performed in 2019. They were the first female K-pop group to perform there.

There's so much more to learn! Make sure to keep up with the latest.

This is Jisoo and actor Lee Min-ho at a photoshoot. They modeled for Samsonite Red. The members of Blackpink do lots of ads.

Fans have their own language. Here are some Blink words you should know:

+ Baby Blinks: Fans can be all ages. Young children like Blackpink. They're called Baby Blinks.
+ Bias: Bias means favorite. Most Blinks have a favorite band member.
+ Blackpink Diaries: These are video blogs. Fans watch these videos on YouTube. Blackpink posts their travels. They post clips of their lives.
+ Comeback: Comebacks mean new song releases. Each comeback has a new theme. Blackpink used to drop their album, songs, and videos at once. But now they release teasers first.
+ Delulu: This word is short for **delusional**. It describes someone who believes things that aren't true. It's used to mock fans. It refers to fans who think they'll date a K-pop idol.
+ Maknae: Maknae refers to the youngest band member. Lisa is the youngest Blackpink.
+ Positions: Positions are roles. Each band member has a job. All band members sing and dance. Jennie, Jisoo, and Rosé are the main singers. Jennie and Lisa are the main rappers. Lisa and Rosé are the main dancers.
+ Visual: Visual is the best-looking band member. Many Blinks say this is Jisoo. But other Blinks disagree.

Blackpink has goals. Lisa said, "Blackpink members and my fans are my driving forces." She always wants to be better. She wants to improve. She said, "I hope people don't know what to expect from us, except for something better than before. We want to be unpredictable." She wants to surprise Blinks. Jennie said she wants to give fans "as much as they gave us."

There are all types of Blackpink fans. They're all around the world. Start your own fan club!

- Promote your fan club.
- Host a meeting.
- Collect a list of names.
- Have fun!
- Plan events.

Blackpink doesn't have an official leader. Jisoo is the oldest. So the others ask her for help.

GLOSSARY

auditioned (aw-DIH-shuhnd) tried out for a role or job by performing

caption (KAP-shuhn) word or sentence that describes an image

celebrities (suh-LEH-bruh-teez) well-known or famous people

climate change (KLYE-muht CHAYNJ) changes in temperature and weather that make Earth warmer and harm the planet

cosplay (KAHZ-play) dress up as a character or famous person

debut (DAY-byoo) first appearance

delusional (dih-LOO-zhuhn-uhl) when someone believes something that is not true

fan base (FAN BAYSS) group of fans for a particular sport, musical group, or celebrity

fandom (FAN-duhm) subculture, community, or network of fans who share a common interest

feminine (FEH-muh-nuhn) having qualities associated with women or girls

idols (EYE-duhlz) people who are greatly admired and loved by others

K-pop (KAY-pahp) South Korean popular culture, including music, movies, TV shows, fashion, and beauty products

merch (MURCH) short for merchandise, which includes posters, shirts, and other items

sasaeng (SAH-sang) South Korean term for an obsessive fan who invades the privacy of Korean idols

savage (SAA-vij) tough or fierce

solo (SOH-loh) performing alone, rather than part of a group

toxic (TAHK-sik) harmful

LEARN MORE

Besley, Adrian. *Blackpink: K-Pop's No. 1 Girl Group*. London: Michael O'Mara, 2023.

Brown, Helen. *Blackpink! Queens of K-Pop*. New York, NY: Sterling Children's Books, 2020.

Stevens, Cara J. *Blackpink: Pretty Isn't Everything*. New York, NY: HarperCollins, 2019.

INDEX